ARITHMETIC

THE FOUNDATION OF

MATHEMATICS

THE STORY OF MATH
Core Principles of Mathematics

ARITHMETIC
THE FOUNDATION OF MATHEMATICS

EDITED BY GARRETT GLADLE

Britannica®
Educational Publishing

IN ASSOCIATION WITH

ROSEN
EDUCATIONAL SERVICES

Published in 2015 by Britannica Educational Publishing (a trademark of Encyclopædia Britannica, Inc.) in association with The Rosen Publishing Group, Inc.
29 East 21st Street, New York, NY 10010

Distributed exclusively by Rosen Publishing.
To see additional Britannica Educational Publishing titles, go to rosenpublishing.com.

First Edition

Britannica Educational Publishing
J.E. Luebering: Director, Core Reference Group
Anthony L. Green: Editor, Compton's by Britannica

Rosen Publishing
Hope Lourie Killcoyne: Executive Editor
Garrett Gladle: Editor
Nelson Sá: Art Director
Brian Garvey: Designer
Cindy Reiman: Photography Manager
Introduction and supplementary material by Barbara Gottfried Hollander.

Library of Congress Cataloging-in-Publication Data

Arithmetic: the foundation of mathematics/edited by Garrett Gladle.—First edition.
 pages cm—(The story of math, core principles of mathematics)
Includes bibliographical references and index.
ISBN 978-1-62275-518-9 (library bound)
1. Arithmetic—Foundations. I. Gladle, Garrett, editor.
QA248.A765 2015
513—dc23

2014017958

Manufactured in the United States of America

Contents

Introduction

I magine a world without numbers. How would someone tell time, determine how far it is to drive to a concert in the next city, find the total cost of a new smartphone, or figure out a bank balance and the interest it has earned? Numbers are part of daily life. Arithmetic is the science of calculating with numbers. People use numbers to measure time, distance, monetary values, and more. Rather than being a course in arithmetic, this resource focuses on its operations.

Consider several goals of a high school student, like making a budget, planning to pay for college, and keeping track of job earnings. All these goals require arithmetic. Budgets involve adding income and subtracting expenses. Finding the cost of college means subtracting financial aid from a school's sticker price. Calculating a bank balance with job wage deposits and interest may use all six basic operations of arithmetic.

The six operations are addition, subtraction, multiplication, division, raising to powers, and finding roots. An example of raising to powers is the use of scientific notation. This notation is a simplified way to write very small or very large numbers, such as expressing distances in the solar system or the number of acres in a town. One sees the use of finding roots in geometry. For example, given the volume of a cube, the length of a side of the cube is found with finding roots.

Arithmetic also encompasses one-to-one correspondence. Putting on shoes is an example of one-to-one correspondence. There is one foot that corresponds, or goes with, one shoe. Making muffins also involves one-to-one correspondence. Bakers put one muffin liner

When making muffins or cupcakes, the baker puts a muffin liner in each cup of the muffin tin, which is an example of one-to-one correspondence. elenaburn/Shutterstock.com

in each muffin tin's cup. In math, a function shows a relationship between one or more variables. A function has one-to-one correspondence because each function output value corresponds to only one input value.

One-to-one correspondence means matching things, like a foot with a shoe. It can also match two numerical values, like in a function. Counting is an arithmetic process that matches things with numbers, like matching pencils in a classroom with numbers that indicate their amounts. The results of this counting exercise help determine if there are enough pencils for each student. People use the counting numbers, or whole numbers beginning at 0, to perform the six basic operations of arithmetic.

Many students use social media. Arithmetic is used to determine how many people visit these sites. When students vote in school, local, state, or national elections, arithmetic finds the winners. Arithmetic is also used to tally scores in sports, like baseball, as well as team activities, like chess tournaments.

Many global organizations provide people in poverty with needed food, medical treatment, housing, and education. These organizations also use arithmetic for such things as finding the number of people who need food or the number of life-saving vaccinations to send.

Arithmetic is one of the most useful of all sciences. It is used throughout the world and our daily lives, making its importance clear. This resource highlights the basic operations in arithmetic, a reminder that all of the simple operations done with numbers would be virtually impossible without it.

Chapter 1

THE BEGINNINGS OF ARITHMETIC

The term *arithmetic* comes from *arithmos*, the Greek word for "number." People began doing arithmetic long before the Greeks invented the word, however, and even before anyone invented numbers.

ONE-TO-ONE CORRESPONDENCE

Historians believe that as early as ten thousand years ago, when prehistoric people started farming, they began to use arithmetic. They needed to know such things as how many sheep they owned, or how many rows of grain they planted, or how long it would be before harvest season arrived.

According to historians, prehistoric farmers devised an ingenious method for keeping track of things; they used a process of matching that

Historians think that prehistoric shepherds figured out a smart system of matching that used pebbles or notches to keep track of every last sheep in their flock. Photos.com/Thinkstock

mathematicians call one-to-one correspondence. A shepherd, for example, could keep track of his flock by dropping a pebble into a pile or by cutting a notch in a twig for every sheep that went to pasture in the morning. He could make sure that all his sheep returned home by matching them, one by one, to the pebbles in his pile or the notches on his twig.

This process of matching pebbles or notches with objects was the first step in the development of arithmetic. In fact, two of the words that people use to describe doing arithmetic, calculating and tallying, come from the Latin words for "pebble" (*calculus*) and "notch" (*taleus*). One-to-one correspondence is still the most basic arithmetic process, and it is so simple that even very young children use it. Before they learn to count, children can often put the right number of forks on the dinner table by laying out "one for mama, one for daddy, one for brother, one for sister, and one for me."

COUNTING

It is just a short step from one-to-one correspondence to counting, which is the process of matching objects with the names of numbers. Counting is the second simplest arithmetic process. The earliest mathematicians, thousands of years ago, probably learned to count in much the same way as little children do today—with their fingers. When a young child wants to show how many people are in his family, he or she might hold up a finger for each family member. The child begins to count by reciting a specific number name for each consecutive finger he or she holds up: "one, two, three, four."

It is not just coincidence that the Latin word for "finger" is *digitus* and that the ten numerals used in writing numbers (0, 1, 2, 3, 4, 5, 6, 7, 8, and 9) are often called digits. The names that people

It's no coincidence that number systems in modern languages, such as English, are based on the number ten, which corresponds to our ten fingers.
© iStockphoto.com/ausinasia

invented for numbers came directly from counting. Most modern languages, including English, have base ten number systems—that is, they have separate number names only for the first ten numbers, corresponding to the ten fingers used for counting. Beyond ten, the cycle of number names begins all over again. For example, in English the word "eleven" comes from the Old English word *endleofan*, which means "one left over." "Twelve" is from the word *twelf*, meaning "two left over." "Thirteen" is clearly a version of "three and ten," and "twenty" comes from the Old English word *twentizh*, which means "two tens."

The numbers that are used for counting—one, two, three, four, and so on—make up a special class of numbers and are referred to as a class by several different terms. They are called counting numbers, whole numbers, or positive integers (from the Latin word *integer*, meaning "whole"). People use these numbers to count whole things, such as one whole apple, two whole days, or three whole words. They are also referred to as natural numbers because they were the first kinds of numbers that occurred to people, and for a long time they were the only numbers that anyone used.

All the laws of arithmetic are based upon these counting, or whole, numbers. When people learn to add, subtract, multiply, divide, raise to powers, and extract roots, they are learning to calculate with whole numbers. Other kinds of numbers, such as fractions, negative integers, and zero, were not introduced until much later, when it was realized that new kinds of numbers were needed to make all the operations of arithmetic possible.

ARITHMETIC OPERATIONS

Arithmetic evolved as a tool to help people

THE HISTORY OF MATHEMATICS

People have used mathematics since ancient times. The Egyptians could not have built the pyramids without a very good understanding of math, especially arithmetic and geometry. The Babylonians of ancient Mesopotamia (now in Iraq) invented a complex number system and used fractions.

The ancient Greeks greatly expanded math with many new ideas. In about 300 BCE, the Greek mathematician Euclid wrote an important book on geometry called *Elements*. Later, the Arabs also contributed greatly to math. In the CE 800s, an Arab mathematician named al-Khwarizmi described a problem-solving system that is now known as algebra.

The ancient Greek and Arab ideas about math eventually spread to Western Europe. Math progressed as European scientists used it to research other subjects. In the 1600s, the astronomer Johannes Kepler used new mathematical ideas to study the skies. Other scientists in the 1600s, namely Galileo and Isaac Newton, applied math to the study of motion. In the 1800s and 1900s, scholars developed many new ways to study and use math.

solve practical problems involving numbers or quantities. Because they had to solve several different kinds of number problems, people had to develop several different kinds of number operations. In arithmetic, the word *operation* refers to a method of combining two numbers

If a mom picks twelve apples, she'll use division to figure out how to equally distribute the fruit among her six children. Andreas Kraus/Shutterstock.com

to get a third. Addition, for example, can solve the problem of how many cows a farmer will have altogether if he buys ten more. Subtraction can solve the problem of how many potatoes a family will have left for tomorrow if they eat six for dinner today. By using multiplication, a woodsman can tell how many trees he will be able to cut in a day if he can cut two in an hour. And division can tell a mother how to split up a basket of twelve apples so that each of her six children gets an equal number.

When arithmetic is used to solve such practical problems, it is called practical, or applied, arithmetic. Early in the history of arithmetic, however, mathematicians discovered that they could deal with numbers that are unrelated to objects. Arithmetic can be used to solve abstract problems, such as $14 + 25 = 39$. By studying abstract problems, or pure arithmetic, mathematicians have isolated certain rules that govern the operations of arithmetic. The following sections will outline the different operations that make up arithmetic and will explain how they developed, how they are used, how they work, and what the laws are that govern them.

2

ADDITION

The process of combining two or more numbers to find the quantity represented by them altogether is called addition. Because addition is so closely related to counting, it was probably the first arithmetic operation that man discovered. Imagine a farmer, thousands of years ago, who found a stray herd of goats. If he combined the stray goats with his own animals, he would probably want to know how many goats he had in all.

One way he could find the number was by counting. If he started out with four goats and found five more, he could count each goat and learn that he had nine altogether. If the farmer counted four and five together often enough, he would soon learn that they always equal nine. He would no longer need to count. He could simply add four and five and know instantly what the answer would be.

At that point the farmer would have learned an addition fact. In school, children who are learning to add often memorize eighty-one of these addition facts:

$$1 + 1 = 2, \quad 1 + 2 = 3, \quad 1 + 3 = 4,$$

all the way to $9 + 9 = 18$.

MORE THAN MEMORIZATION

But no one can memorize the answer to every possible addition problem; some are too complex. For example, it would not be easy to know automatically the total of 87 and 45, and it would take too long to count that number of objects. In ancient times there was no easy way to compute addition problems in writing. Even though people began writing numbers as early as five thousand years ago, ancient systems of written numbers were too cumbersome to use for calculating. Adding 87 and 45 in Roman numerals would mean adding LXXXVII and XLV. Even in Roman times, only special scribes could perform this feat. Roman and Greek numeration systems used letters to represent numbers. The letters were useful for recording, but they were not useful for adding.

Many ancient peoples used a simple mechanical calculating device called an abacus. On an abacus, each vertical column has room for many pebbles. The pebbles in the column farthest to the right represent units, or ones. Those in the next column stand for tens, then hundreds, and so on.

Adding 87 and 45 on an abacus is easy. First the pebbles presenting 87 are placed in the proper columns. (This number is called the augend, which means "supposed to be

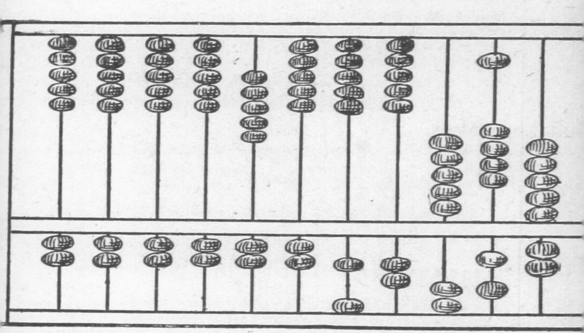

An abacus was a basic mechanical tool used by ancient peoples for making calculations by moving counters along rods or in grooves. The British Library

increased.") Then the pebbles representing 45 are added to them. (The number to be added is called the addend.) The combined total, or the sum, usually needs abbreviating, which is done by regrouping. Ten pebbles in any column can be replaced by one pebble in the column to its left. The replacement is called a carry.

ABACUS: THE EARLIEST CALCULATOR

Long before the invention of the electronic calculator or the computer, people counted and did calculations with a device called an abacus. On this instrument, calculations are made with beads, or counters, instead of numerals. The beads are arranged on wires stretched across a frame. Each wire represents the ones, tens, hundreds, and so on.

The abacus was probably invented by an ancient group of people known as Sumerians in Mesopotamia. The ancient Egyptians, Greeks, Romans, Hindus, and Chinese all used the abacus as well.

In about 700 CE, the Hindus invented a numeral system that made adding with written numbers as easy as adding on an abacus. The Arabs soon adopted this system, and they introduced it into Europe more than one thousand years ago. As written calculations became easier, the abacus passed out of use in Europe. But it continues to be used by people living in China, Japan, and the Middle East.

ARABIC NUMERALS

In approximately 700 CE, the Hindus of India invented a numeral system that made adding with written numbers as easy as adding on an abacus. The Arabs soon adopted this number system, and in 1202 the discovery reached Europe by way of an Italian mathematician, Leonardo Fibonacci. The new system, called Arabic numerals, simplified written addition and other calculations so dramatically that none better has been found and it is still in use.

Why are Arabic numerals so easy to use? The answer is that they are modeled on the abacus. Like the abacus, the Arabic numeral system is a decimal system; that is, it groups numbers by tens. The Hindus originally invented nine different symbols, corresponding to the nine pebbles used in each column of the abacus. These symbols changed shape over the years, but when printing was invented in the 15th century, the symbols became standardized: 1, 2, 3, 4, 5, 6, 7, 8, 9.

The Arabic number system can use these nine symbols to represent very large numbers because the system is positional: A numeral's position determines its value. In the Arabic

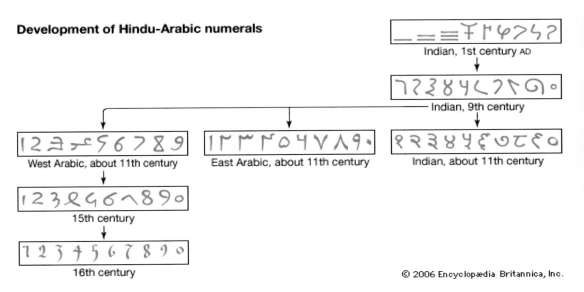

Development of Hindu-Arabic numerals

Indian, 1st century AD

Indian, 9th century

West Arabic, about 11th century

East Arabic, about 11th century

Indian, about 11th century

15th century

16th century

© 2006 Encyclopædia Britannica, Inc.

Hindu-Arabic numerals are now used in most of the countries of the world. People who write in the Arabic alphabet still use an older form of Hindu-Arabic numerals called East Arabic numerals. Encyclopædia Britannica, Inc.

system, as on an abacus, a nine in the ones column means nine, but a nine in the tens column means ninety, and in the hundreds column it means nine hundred.

ADD IN ZERO

Eventually the Hindus had to invent a new symbol to stand for an empty column on the abacus. The concept of zero and symbol o are taken for granted today; but until the Hindus invented it around 700 CE, no number system had found an easy way to distinguish between 17, 107, and 1,070. The invention of zero revolutionized arithmetic.

When people add, they use Arabic numerals to represent the quantities they want to combine. By adding the numerals together in much the same way that pebbles are added together on the abacus, people get the same answer as if they had actually counted objects one by one.

WHO CARES ABOUT ORDER?

In the course of adding with numbers, mathematicians discovered two fundamental laws about addition. First, the order in which numbers are added never affects the sum:

$3 + 6 = 9$ and $6 + 3 = 9$;

$7 + 3 + 6 = 16$ and $6 + 7 + 3 = 16$.

Mathematicians have called this property the commutative law of addition because the numbers can commute, or change places, but not change their total value. To show that the law is true for all addition problems, mathematicians illustrate it with letters rather than numbers:

$$a + b = b + a$$

The other fundamental property of addition that mathematicians discovered is this: when someone is adding more than two numbers, it makes no difference in what order the numbers are added. $1 + 2 + 3$ can be added together in several different orders and still give the same sum. To show which numbers should be combined first, mathematicians enclose them in parentheses:

So, $1 + (2 + 3) = 1 + 5 = 6$

and $(1 + 2) + 3 = 3 + 3 = 6$.

Mathematicians refer to this property as the associative law of addition, indicating that the numbers can associate in different orders. They illustrate the law:

$$(a + b) + c = a + (b + c)$$

Those who have been doing arithmetic for a long time may wonder why these laws are worth noting. It seems obvious that $1 + 2 = 2 + 1$

and that $(1+2)+3 = 1+(2+3)$. But not every process of addition is commutative and associative. In chemistry, for instance, the order in which chemicals are added often makes a great deal of difference to the result. If sulfuric acid is added to water (water + sulfuric acid), the result will be dilute sulfuric acid. If water is added to the acid (sulfuric acid + water), the result can be an explosion. Only in arithmetic is addition always commutative and associative.

It is only in arithmetic that addition is both commutative and associative. Adding ingredients in a random order during a chemistry experiment may cause an unanticipated explosion. © iStockphoto.com/Kali Nine LLC

These laws are also worth considering because they help explain why the commonly used methods of addition work. For example, they help explain how numbers can be switched to simplify addition: $20+6+90$ can be switched by the commutative law to $20+90+6$. By the associative law, $20+90$ can be combined first, so $(20+90)+6=110+6=116$.

The laws also help explain how the column addition method works. When $41+15+72$ are added together, the addition looks like this:

$$\begin{array}{r} 41 \\ 15 \\ +72 \\ \hline 128 \end{array}$$

As the numbers are added, what actually happens is that all the ones are grouped together and added first; then all the tens are grouped and added. In other words $41+15+72$ is broken down to $(40+1)+(10+5)+(70+2)$. The numbers are regrouped by the associative law:

$$(40+10+70)+(1+5+2)=120+8=128$$

SUBTRACTION

Although many people choose to think of subtraction as a separate and distinct arithmetic process, it is not. Subtraction is just the reverse of addition.

Primitive people probably needed subtraction to solve basic problems as much as they needed addition. If a prehistoric father picked an armful of fourteen apples to feed his family of ten and he dropped four apples, he would want to know how many he had left to feed his family. Or if he had collected only four apples, he might want to know how many more he would need to feed everyone at home.

Subtraction answers both kinds of questions. When a number of things are taken away, subtraction answers how many things are left. And if two quantities are being

If your basket of twenty tomatoes topples over and seven fall out, you'll use subtraction to figure out how many you still have left. RoJo Images/ Shutterstock.com

compared, subtraction answers how many more are needed to make them equal or what the difference is between the two.

SUBTRACTION BY COUNTING

Like addition, subtraction can be done by counting. The apple picker could hold up four fingers and then count the remaining fingers on his hand to see how many more he needed to reach ten. Once he learned that $10 - 4$ always equals 6, he would have learned a subtraction fact. If he memorized eighty-one of these subtraction facts, he would be prepared with answers for most of his daily subtraction problems. But when people began to face more complicated subtraction problems, they required some subtraction procedure that would be more practical than either counting or memorizing.

In ancient times, most complicated subtraction was probably done on an abacus. If an abacus has pebbles representing 7,438, it is easy to subtract 5,236 by taking away five pebbles from the thousands column, two from the hundreds, three from the tens and six from the ones.

Subtracting in the Arabic numeral system follows much the same process as abacus subtraction. The problem 7,214 minus 5,236 can be written

7000 and 200 and 10 and 4

minus

5000 and 200 and 30 and 6

Because six cannot be subtracted from four, or thirty from ten, numbers have to be borrowed; the top numbers have to be regrouped and rewritten. After the regrouping, the problem would look like this:

```
        6000 and 1100 and 100 and 14
minus   5000 and  200 and  30 and  6
        1000 and  900 and  70 and  8 or 1,978.
```

LESS THAN ZERO

The process of borrowing and regrouping helped solve some sticky subtraction complications. Other complications were more difficult to solve. How, for example, can five be subtracted from four? Some ancient mathematicians declared it could not be done because $4-5$ would be less than nothing. It was not until the 16th century that the Italian mathematician Girolamo Cardano first began to use numbers less than zero.

GIROLAMO CARDANO

Italian Renaissance mathematician, astrologer, and physician Girolamo Cardano wrote more than 130 books on topics ranging from anatomy to philosophy. Cardano was born on Sept. 24, 1501, in Pavia in the Duchy of Milan (now in Italy). He gambled to pay his way through university medical studies at Pavia and Padua. Calculating odds to win at cards or dice led to his *Liber de ludo aleae* (*The Book on Games of Chance*), the first systematic computation of probabilities.

Cardano was the leading mathematician of his time. In *Ars magna* (*The Great Art*; or, *The Rules of Algebra*), published in 1545, he introduced the concept of imaginary numbers and revealed a way to find the roots of cubic equations, still called "Cardano's solution." The book infuriated Venetian mathematician Niccolò Tartaglia, who had told him the cubic solution and sworn him to secrecy. Cardano responded that he had found the solution in an earlier work by someone else, so he did not feel bound by his promise to Tartaglia. His *Ars magna* is one of the cornerstones in the history of algebra.

Cardano put to use what his predecessor Leonardo Fibonacci had recognized three centuries earlier: There can be an amount smaller than zero—for example, a debt. If someone had six dollars and paid it toward a nine-dollar debt, he would still owe three dollars. In subtraction that problem could be written $6 - 9 = -3$. Because subtraction is indicated by a minus sign (−), numbers less than zero are marked with that sign also.

Early mathematicians recognized the usefulness of numbers less than zero but were not happy about having to use them. They gave these numbers the unflattering name *negatives* from the Latin word meaning "to

When the thermometer on a winter morning reads −5 degrees, we know the air needs to get five degrees warmer before the temperature is zero again. victorass/Shutterstock.com

deny." Two more appropriate terms for negative numbers are *additive inverse* and *opposite*. As these names suggest, all negative numbers require an equal and opposite amount to be added to them to give zero. A debt of five dollars requires payment of five dollars before the account is cleared. An air temperature of −5 degrees requires the air to get five degrees warmer before the temperature reaches zero. In other words $-5 + 5 = 0$ just as $5 - 5 = 0$. This view of negative numbers suggests another way to understand subtraction. Subtracting any number is the same as adding its opposite:

$$a - b = a + (-b)$$

MULTIPLICATION

When people learned to add, they had developed a time-saving device. Addition is just a shortcut method of counting, but even addition can be time-consuming, especially when the same number must be added repeatedly. Situations requiring repeated addition must have arisen often, even in ancient times. If a shepherd wanted to trade sixteen of his sheep for a supply of wheat, and if each sheep was worth twenty-nine bushels of wheat, the shepherd would have to add sixteen 29s to calculate his price. Ancient mathematicians developed multiplication to simplify repeated addition problems.

DOUBLE, DOUBLE

One of the earliest multiplication techniques was called doubling or duplation. The

Multiplication was developed by early mathematicians to make repeated addition problems, such as determining how many bushels of hay to trade for one sheep, much simpler. Bartosz Zakrzewski/Shutterstock.com

shepherd who had to add sixteen 29s probably began by adding 29 + 29 to get 58; but he may have recognized that eight 58s would give the same sum as sixteen 29s. Probably much encouraged, he added again: 58 + 58 = 116. Could the eight 58s be replaced by four 116s? Yes, and the four 116s could be replaced by two 232s, which gave the sum 464. The whole problem could be done by four doublings instead of sixteen additions—quite a time-saver.

The multiplication technique used today is faster than doubling. It is a mechanical method of manipulating numbers that can be used to calculate the sum of large numbers but only requires two digits to be multiplied at a time.

X	1	2	3	4	5	6	7	8	9	10
1	1	2	3	4	5	6	7	8	9	10
2	2	4	6	8	10	12	14	16	18	20
3	3	6	9	12	15	18	21	24	27	30
4	4	8	12	16	20	24	28	32	36	40
5	5	10	15	20	25	30	35	40	45	50
6	6	12	18	24	30	36	42	48	54	60
7	7	14	21	28	35	42	49	56	63	70
8	8	16	24	32	40	48	56	64	72	80
9	9	18	27	36	45	54	63	72	81	90
10	10	20	30	40	50	60	70	80	90	100

Thanks to the handy multiplication table, shown here, multiplying large numbers can be done very quickly. Sufi/Shutterstock.com

In order to multiply quickly, it is necessary only to memorize all the possible multiplications of two digits, from 1 × 1 = 1 to 9 × 9 = 81. These are called multiplication facts or the multiplication table. The sign "×" is read "times," and the problem 9 × 9 actually means nine added nine times. The answer to this multiplication problem, 81, is called the product. One additional multiplication fact must also be remembered: Any number multiplied by zero equals zero. This fact makes sense because 3 × 0 actually means 0 added three times, a process that would result in zero.

WHY MULTIPLY?

Arithmetic textbooks teach the multiplication technique thoroughly. Many people, however, have lost touch with the principle behind multiplication—why the technique works. The problem 29 × 26 can serve to illustrate the principle. Worked out by the standard multiplication method, the problem will look like this:

$$
\begin{array}{r}
26 \\
\times\ 29 \\
\hline
234 \\
52\ \ \\
\hline
754
\end{array}
$$

It is easier to see what is actually happening if the two numbers to be multiplied (called multiplicands) are broken down into their positional components:

$$\begin{array}{r} 20 \text{ and } 6 \\ \times\, 20 \text{ and } 9 \\ \hline \end{array}$$

Each of the components on the top line is multiplied by each of the components, on the bottom line; after this is done, all the answers (called partial products) are added up.

$$\begin{array}{r} 20 \text{ and } 6 \\ \times\, 20 \text{ and } 9 \\ \hline 54 \\ 180 \\ 120 \\ 400 \\ \hline 754 \end{array}$$

This method of multiplication works because multiplication is distributive. In other words, when the sums of numbers are multiplied, all the multiplications are distributed evenly. Each of the addends of one sum is multiplied by each of the addends of the other sum. To illustrate, 5×5, which equals 25, can be broken down into the product of two sums, $(2+3) \times (4+1)$. According to the distributive law, the sums are multiplied in the following way:

$$(2+3) \times (4+1) =$$

$$(2 \times 4) + (2 \times 1) + (3 \times 4) + (3 \times 1) =$$

ADJUSTABLE ALGEBRA

With algebra and basic arithmetic—addition, subtraction, multiplication, and division—it is possible to solve almost any equation that has a variable. Algebra is a method of thinking about mathematics in a general way. It provides rules about how equations must be put together and how they can be changed. The word *algebra* comes from the title of a book on mathematics written in the early 800s by an Arab astronomer and mathematician named al-Khwarizmi. The rules of algebra are older than that, however. The ancient Greeks wrote down some of the rules that make up algebra, and others came later.

Mathematicians have found that the easiest way to write down the general rules of algebra is to use what are called variables. Variables are symbols (usually letters like a, b, x, y) that represent, or take the place of, either any number or an unknown number. For example, one of the rules of algebra says that $a + b = b + a$. In this case, a and b are variables that represent any numbers. The rule is true no matter what numbers the letters represent. If $a = 3$ and $b = 2$ or if $a = 246$ and $b = 912$, the rule is still true. That is, $3 + 2 = 2 + 3$ and $246 + 912 = 912 + 246$, and so on.

An important branch of mathematics, algebra today is studied not only in high school and college but, increasingly, in the lower grades as well. Taught with insight and understanding of the new mathematics programs, it can be an enjoyable subject. Algebra is as useful as all the other branches of mathematics—to which it is closely related. For some careers, such as those in engineering and science, a knowledge of algebra is indispensable.

$$8 + 2 + 12 + 3 = 25$$

Mathematicians illustrate the distributive law

$$a(b + c) = (ab) + (ac)$$

Because multiplication is a shortened form of addition, it has two other fundamental properties that it shares with addition. Multiplication is both commutative and associative. According to the commutative law of multiplication, $ab = ba$, the order in which numbers are multiplied never affects their product: $4 \times 5 = 20$ and $5 \times 4 = 20$. According to the associative law, $ab(c) = a(bc)$, when someone is multiplying more than two numbers, it makes no difference in what order the numbers are multiplied:

$$8(2 \times 9) = 8 \times 18 = 144$$

and $(8 \times 2) \times 9 = 16 \times 9 = 144$

DIVISION

Although multiplication combines numbers to obtain sums, division separates numbers into equal parts. Division is the opposite of multiplication—multiplication is a shortened method of adding, and division is a shortened method of subtracting.

BACKWARD THINKING

One of the difficulties in learning division is understanding that it is really a process that works backward. Rather than learning division facts, one must learn to apply multiplication facts in reverse. The problem "What is 18 ÷ 3?" is the same as asking: "What number times 3 equals 18?" According to the multiplication table, the answer is 6.

Some examples can illustrate exactly how division is related to both multiplication and subtraction. Division can solve the problem of how to split twelve apples into three equal groups. This problem calls for a kind of back-ward multiplication: 3 × ? apples = 12 apples. The answer that you get, according to the multiplica-tion table, is 4.

Division can also solve another kind of prob-lem: If the milk filling a twelve-quart container has to be transferred to three-quart containers, how many three-quart containers will be filled? This problem may be worked out literally with cans. The milk from the twelve-quart container

One way to use division is to figure out how many six-ounce glasses can be filled from a thirty-six-ounce pitcher of lemonade. © iStockphoto.com/ kyoshino

can be poured to fill one three-quart can, then a second three-quart can, then a third can, and a fourth can. This problem in effect calls for a kind of repeated subtraction—subtracting three quarts of milk four times.

Both problems pose the question, "How many times does 3 go into 12?" and both problems are written 12 ÷ 3 = 4 (12 divided by 3 equals 4). The number to the left of the division sign, 12, is called the dividend; the number to the right, 3, is called the divisor; and the answer to the problem, 4, is called the quotient, derived from the Latin word meaning "how many times."

Long division is commonly used to solve complicated problems, and it is a mechanical process of unmultiplying. In this example, long division repeats a cycle of guess-multiply-subtract until the problem is solved.

$$
\begin{array}{r}
21487 \\
12\overline{)257844} \\
24 \\
\hline
17 \\
12 \\
\hline
58 \\
48 \\
\hline
104 \\
96 \\
\hline
84 \\
84 \\
\hline
0
\end{array}
$$

Solving this problem requires (1) guessing "What number times 12 equals 25?"; (2) multiplying the answer, 2, by 12; and (3) subtracting that answer, 24, from 25. The next digit is dropped down, and the cycle repeats until the entire problem is unmultiplied and the last subtraction yields zero.

Most division problems do not end so neatly in a zero. What happens, for instance, when 175 is divided by 2? There is no exact whole number that can be multiplied by 2 to give 175. The closest is 87: 2 times 87 is 174 and 1 is left over. It would be extremely impractical for mathematicians to avoid this type of problem because it does not come out evenly. It is often necessary to divide such numbers.

BROKEN UP: FRACTIONS

If a father insists upon dividing his 175 acres of land equally between his two children, he would give each of them 87 acres and a half of the remaining acre. To deal with division problems that do not yield whole numbers, mathematicians have developed a kind of number to represent a part of a whole unit: the fraction.

People have been using fractions since ancient times. The Rhind papyrus, an

Egyptian mathematical document written about 1650 BCE, makes use of fractions in which the numerator (the top number) is one: ¼, ½, and so on. It is easy to see why fractions were discovered at almost the same time as whole numbers. People began using whole numbers as soon as they found it necessary to count, and they used whole numbers to count separate and individual objects.

Numbers were needed not only for counting but also for measuring. People had to measure land area and distance, food, and time. Land and food and time do not always exist in evenly measurable amounts. A farmer may own only a part of an acre of land. An activity may last for some amount of time less than an hour. Early in history, people needed numbers smaller than whole numbers.

At first only the simplest fractions were used. People tried to avoid more complex fractions whenever possible by subdividing their units of measurement into smaller units. An hour, for instance, is divided into 60 subunits called minutes. A foot is divided into 12 subunits called inches. A circle is divided into 360 subunits called degrees.

The reason that 12, 60, and 360 appear so often as numbers of subunits is that each of these numbers has several factors—that is,

The Rhind papyrus, which uses fractions like ½ and ¼, dates back to about 1650 BCE. DeAgostini/SuperStock

several numbers can be divided into them evenly without leaving fractions. Twelve, for instance, can be divided evenly by 1, 2, 3, 4, 6, and 12.

There are many occasions when units must be divided into parts. If two acres of land must be divided into three equal portions, each portion will be smaller than one acre. The size of each portion is represented by the fraction 2/3, which is read as "two thirds," or "two over three," or "two divided by three." A fraction is actually a compact division problem, and any division problem can be represented as a fraction. The parent who needed to divide his 175 acres between 2 children would divide 175 by 2 and give each of them 175/2 acres or 87½ acres.

DIGGING THE DECIMAL

Calculating with fractions was originally more complicated than calculating with integers because fractions did not fit neatly into the positional notation system. By the 17th century, however, people began to use a positional method for representing portions of whole numbers—decimal fractions.

Any fraction written as a division (3/4, 11/12, 29/72, etc.) can be converted to a

CHANGE FOR A DOLLAR: FRACTIONS

There are many ways to make change for a dollar: two half-dollars, four quarters, ten dimes, twenty nickels, or one hundred pennies. No matter how the change is made, the dollar is broken up—"fractured"—into several pieces. These pieces are called fractions, from the same Latin word (*fractus*, meaning "broken") that fracture comes from.

All fractions represent parts of a whole. It has long been convenient and customary to divide things into segments. Hours are divided into sixty minutes each. Days are divided into twenty-four hours and years into twelve months. Miles are divided into feet and kilometers into meters. Each of these segments can be expressed as a fraction. One inch is one twelve part, or one-twelfth, of a foot. Fractions are very helpful because they make possible measurements in other than whole numbers such as 1, 2, or 5. Measurements with fractions can often be more precise: It is more exact to say "four and one-tenth gallons" than "a little more than four gallons."

decimal fraction by dividing the numerator by the denominator. To convert 3/4 into a decimal fraction, three is divided by four, and a decimal point is used to separate any integers from the fraction:

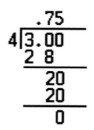

The major advantage in using the decimal system is that decimal fractions can be added, subtracted, multiplied, and divided exactly as whole numbers can.

REPEAT AFTER ME

The process of repeating the multiplication of a number, or raising that number to a certain power, was once known as involution. The reverse is a process called evolution, which is a process of repeated division. Although both terms were popular in the 19th century, both have since fallen out of favor.

MULTIPLE MULTIPLICATION

The process of simplifying arithmetic calculations continues beyond the process of multiplication. When multiplication is viewed as a shortened form of arithmetic, it seems like a great advance. But even figuring out the product of a simple multiplication problem like $15 \times 15 \times 15$ requires a significant amount of work:

$$
\begin{array}{rr}
15 & 225 \\
\times 15 & \times\ 15 \\
\hline
75 & 1125 \\
15 & 225 \\
\hline
225 & 3375
\end{array}
$$

MORE MULTIPLICATION

Repeated multiplications often arise in arithmetic. To calculate the volume of a cube with a three-foot edge, for example, the length of the edge must be multiplied three times: $3 \times 3 \times 3 = 27$ cubic feet. René Descartes, the father of modern mathematics, adopted a shorthand notation. He used a new type of symbol called an exponent. In exponential notation 8×8 is written as 8^2. The small number above the line, the exponent, indicates the number of times the base number, 8, is to be multiplied, or used as a factor. The process of repeating the multiplication of a number involves raising that number to a certain power. So $14 \times 14 \times 14 \times 14 \times 14$ is written 14^5 and is called 14 to the fifth power.

CALCULATING MADE EASY

Exponential numbers are useful to arithmetic in an important way: They provide an easy

René Descartes. Photos.com/Thinkstock

RENÉ DESCARTES

René Descartes (1596–1650) was born on March 31, 1596, at La Haye (now Descartes), in the Touraine region of France. Both modern philosophy and modern mathematics began with the work of René Descartes. He attempted to justify certain basic beliefs about human beings, the world, and God using a technique of systematic doubt that he invented. He also developed the first modern theory that mind and body are essentially different substances, a distinction that has occupied philosophers ever since. His invention of analytic, or coordinate, geometry prepared the way for further advances in mathematics. He also insisted that knowledge in the sciences should be based not on probabilities but on certainties derived from observations and experiments.

It was in 1619 that Descartes developed analytic geometry, in which points are represented as pairs of numbers and lines and curves are represented as algebraic equations. This allows geometric problems to be solved with algebra. In that same year, he concluded that the universe has a mathematically logical structure and that a single method of reasoning, based on mathematics, could apply to all natural sciences. His method involved accepting as true only that which is self-evident; breaking down a problem into its simplest parts; systematically deducing one conclusion from another, moving from simple to complex; and rechecking the reasoning.

method to calculate with very large numbers. Scientists and mathematicians have adopted the practice of expressing very large numbers in exponential form—especially as powers of 10. The number representing the speed of light—30,000,000,000 centimeters per second—is written by scientists as 3×10^{10}. Suppose the scientist wanted to find out how far light had traveled in 100,000,000 seconds. Standard multiplication techniques would result in a huge number. But the scientist can multiply with the exponential numbers. The rule for multiplying with exponents is: To multiply two powers with the same base, add the exponents and use their sum as the exponent of the common base. The scientist's problem would look like this:

$$3 \times 10^{10} \times 10^{8} = 3 \times 10^{18}$$

Dividing exponential numbers calls for subtracting the exponents: $3^{4} \div 3^{2} = 3^{2}$. Working through this problem will illustrate this rule:

$$3^{4} \div 3^{2} =$$

$$(3 \times 3 \times 3 \times 3)/(3 \times 3) =$$

$$81/9 =$$

$$9 = 3^2$$

Exponents can be used to represent extremely small numbers and fractions. Use the rule for dividing exponents: $3^2 \div 3^3 = 3^{-1}$. If these numbers are represented in the standard Arabic numeral form, the problem would read $9 \div 27$ or $9/27$ or $1/3$. So 3^{-1} actually equals $1/3$. The negative exponent signals that the exponential number is a fraction.

ROOTING OUT THE ROOT

Every arithmetic operation has its reverse. The reverse of addition is subtraction. The reverse of multiplication is division. And the reverse of finding the power is finding the root. Since finding the power is a process of repeated multiplication, it stands to reason that finding the root is a process of repeated division. This process of repeated division leads to finding the foundation, called the root, of a number. If the number 64 is divided by 4 three times, the answer will be 1:

$$64 \div 4 = 16$$

$$16 \div 4 = 4$$

$4 \div 4 = 1$

Four is the third root of 64 and is written as

$$\sqrt[3]{64}$$

People are not called upon to work out roots very often, and the method is too complicated to use unnecessarily. Fortunately mathematicians have developed an alternative notation that simplifies calculating with roots. They represent roots as fractional exponents. The square root (or second root) of 16 can be written as either

$$\sqrt{16} \qquad 16^{1/2}$$

In both cases, the number equals 4.

Fractional exponents, like regular fractions, can be converted to decimal form:

$$16^{1/2} = 16^{.5}$$

Once these equivalences were worked out, it became possible to express all the real numbers in a similar exponential form.

In the early 17th century, a Scottish mathematician, John Napier, and a British mathematician, Henry Briggs, developed a

CARL FRIEDRICH GAUSS

The German scientist and mathematician Carl Friedrich Gauss (1777–1855) is frequently called the founder of modern mathematics. His work in astronomy and physics is nearly as significant as that in mathematics.

Many anecdotes refer to his extraordinary feats of mental computation. As an old man, he said jokingly that he could count before he could talk. In elementary school, he quickly impressed his teacher, who is said to have convinced Gauss's father that the son should be permitted to study with a view toward entering a university. In secondary school, after 1788, he rapidly distinguished himself in ancient languages and mathematics.

At the age of 14, Gauss was presented to the duke of Brunswick at court, where he was permitted to exhibit his computing skill. The duke was so impressed that he generously supported Gauss until the duke's death in 1806.

In 1791, Gauss began to do totally new and innovative work in mathematics. In 1793–94, he did intensive research in number theory, especially on prime numbers. He made this his life's passion and is regarded as its modern founder.

He was well versed in the Greek and Roman classics, studied Sanskrit, and read extensively in European literature. In later years he was showered with honors from scientific bodies and governments everywhere. He died in Göttingen on Feb. 23, 1855.

system that put the properties of exponents to their most practical use and greatly simplified arithmetic. They invented a system of logarithms. A logarithm is an exponent. Napier discovered that if every possible number could be expressed as a power of a common base, then all problems of multiplication and division could be reduced to problems of adding and subtracting exponents. Briggs suggested that this common base be ten. He created a table that recorded the log (or power of ten) for every number. The log for 100 is 2, which stands for 10^2. Numbers that are not natural powers of 10 are represented in the table by decimal logs. The log of 1,074 equals 3.0311 because $1,074 = 10\textasciicircum 3.0311$.

Conclusion

Since the advent of electronic computers and pocket calculators, complicated arithmetic operations are accomplished much more easily. Even scientific calculators can almost always be within reach, on the smartphones, tablets, and laptops many people carry with them wherever they go. Raising to powers, figuring roots, and calculating logs can be done in a matter of seconds with a calculator nearly anywhere and at any time.

It's easy to take these quick calculations for granted. The history of the development of arithmetic might seem like something to skim, too, but a closer read reveals an interesting story that's difficult to put down. And it is still necessary to know what the operations of arithmetic are to be able to use them correctly for the many purposes that they serve. Addition, subtraction, multiplication, division, raising powers, and finding roots are

$a^2 + b^2 = c^2$

$Sin = \dfrac{opposite}{hyp}$

$cos = \dfrac{adjacent}{hyp}$

$Tan = \dfrac{opposite}{adjacent}$

Tan^{-1}

Electronic calculators certainly make difficult calculations much easier, but there is no substitute for knowing the basic operations of arithmetic.
Purestock/Thinkstock

used in all other branches of mathematics; a reminder that without arithmetic, geometry, algebra, and calculus would not be possible.

Glossary

abacus A device used for counting and calculating by sliding small balls or beads along rods or in grooves.

addend A number that is to be added to another.

associative Of, having, or being the property of producing the same mathematical value no matter how an expression's elements are grouped.

carry A quantity that is transferred in addition from one number place to the one of next higher place value.

commutative Of, relating to, having, or being the property of giving the same mathematical result no matter in which order two numbers are used with an operation.

correspondence A relation between sets in which each member of one set is matched to one or more members of the other set.

decimal system A system of measurement or money in which each basic unit is ten times larger than the next smaller unit.

dividend A number to be divided by another.

divisor The number by which a dividend is divided.

exponent A symbol written above and to the right of a mathematical expression to mean raising that expression to the power of the symbol.

function A mathematical relationship that assigns exactly one element of one set to each element of the same or another set.

integers Numbers that are natural numbers (as 1, 2, or 3); the negative of a natural number, or 0—also called whole numbers.

multiplicands Numbers that are to be multiplied by others.

numerator The part of a fraction that is above the line and signifies the number to be divided by the denominator.

product The number or expression resulting from the multiplication of two or more numbers or expressions.

quotient The number resulting from the division of one number by another.

sum The result of adding numbers.

variables Quantities that may take on any one of a set of values.

velocity The speed of an object in a specific direction.

For More Information

American Mathematical Society (AMS)
201 Charles Street
Providence, RI 02904
(800) 321-4AMS
Website: http://www.ams.org
The American Mathematical Society was
founded in 1888 to promote mathematical research and scholarship for all ages
and levels all over the world. Among other
goals, the AMS seeks to increase the
awareness of mathematics and its relation-
ships to other fields and daily life.

Association for Women in Mathematics
(AWM)
11240 Waples Mill Road, Suite 200
Fairfax, VA 22030
(703) 934-0163
Website: http://www.awm-math.org
The nonprofit Association for Women in
Mathematics organization was founded in
1971. The AWM strives to inspire women
and girls to study math as well as to seek
careers in the mathematical science fields.

Canadian Mathematical Society
209 - 1725 St. Laurent Boulevard
Ottawa, ON K1G 3V4
Canada

(613) 733-2662

Website: http://cms.math.ca

Originally founded as the Canadian
Mathematical Congress in 1945, the
focus of the Canadian Mathematical
Society is "to promote and advance the
discovery, learning and application of
mathematics."

MATHCOUNTS Foundation

1420 King Street

Alexandria, VA 22314

(703) 299-9006

Website: http://mathcounts.org

The MATHCOUNTS Foundation is a nonprofit organization that strives to encourage
middle school students to view math as fun
and challenging. It seeks to broaden their
mathematical opportunities in school as well
as in future professional lives.

Mathematical Association of America (MAA)

1529 18th Street NW

Washington, DC 20036-1358

(800) 741-9415

Website: http://www.maa.org

The Mathematical Association of America
is the largest professional society that
concentrates on mathematics at levels

understandable to undergraduates. The MAA is open to anyone interested in mathematical sciences.

Mathematical Staircase, Inc.
278 Bay Road
Hadley, MA 01035
Website: http://www.mathstaircase.org
Mathematical Staircase, Inc., is a nonprofit organization based in Massachusetts. Its goal is to provide education for mathematically inclined students, especially those who would otherwise lack the resources to do so.

Pacific Institute for the Mathematical Sciences (PIMS)
PIMS - UBC Site Office
University of British Columbia
4176-2207 Main Mall
Vancouver, BC V6T 1Z4
Canada
(604) 822-3922
Website: http://www.pims.math.ca
In 1996, a group of mathematical scientists in Alberta and British Columbia created the Pacific Institute for the Mathematical Sciences. Today, the organization extends to Washington State and Saskatchewan

in its endeavors to promote research in the mathematical sciences, as well as to train personnel, and highlight public awareness of education in the mathematical sciences.

WEBSITES

Because of the changing nature of Internet links, Rosen Publishing has developed an online list of websites related to the subject of this book. This site is updated regularly. Please use this link to access the list:

http://www.rosenlinks.com/MATH/Arith

Ball, Johnny. *Why Pi?* New York, NY: DK Publishing, 2009.

Barrow, John D. *100 Essential Things You Didn't Know You Didn't Know: Math Explains Your World.* New York, NY: W.W. Norton, 2009.

Canavan, Thomas, Jr. *Math Standards Workout: Computation Skills: 50 Math Super Puzzles.* New York, NY: Rosen Central, 2011.

Frary, Mark. *Mathematics Explained* (The Guide for Curious Minds). New York, NY: Rosen Publishing: 2014.

Gregersen, Erik. *The Britannica Guide to the History of Mathematics.* New York, NY: Britannica Educational Publishing, 2010.

Hosch, William L. *The Britannica Guide to Algebra and Trigonometry.* New York, NY: Rosen Education Service, 2010.

Hosch, William L. *The Britannica Guide to Numbers and Measurement.* New York, NY: Rosen Education Service, 2010.

Jackson, Tom, ed. *Mathematics: An Illustrated History of Numbers.* New York, NY: Shelter Harbor Press, 2012.

Katz, Brian P., and Michael Starbird. *Distilling Ideas: An Introduction to Mathematical Thinking.* Washington, DC: Mathematical Association of America, 2013.

Pickover, Clifford A. *The Math Book: From Pythagoras to the 57th Dimension, 250 Milestones in the History of Mathematics.* New York, NY: Sterling, 2012.

Reimer, David. *Count Like an Egyptian.* Princeton, NJ: Princeton Univeristy, 2014.

Rogers, Kirsteen, Tori Large, Ruth Russell, and Karen Tomlins. *Illustrated Elementary Math Dictionary.* London, England: Usborne, 2010.

Rooney, Anne. *The History of Mathematics.* New York, NY: Rosen Publishing, 2012.